The ABC's of Being Human

The ABC's of Being Human

from the heart-mind of
Penni Sparks

Images by
Alexander Orion Sparks
& Penni Sparks

Wordsmithed by
Kim Dunn

November 2020

First Printing November 2020

ISBN 9798573635910 (paperback)

This book is dedicated to

the still, small voice within

who keeps getting stronger every day.

Thank you for my life.

Appreciations

Thank you to all who practice peace and choose kindness;
To all who take the courageous step to wake up to
their own flaws and choose to gently do better;
To all who offer a smile, a greeting, or a hand;
To all who have inconvenienced themselves for another, and to
all who have asked for help
when it may have inconvenienced another;
To all who have welcomed me into their homes, their hearts,
and their lives—I've been observing and learning
from your choices and from mine throughout my life.
My heart is so full. Thank you.

Specifically, thank you to Kim Dunn
who wordsmithed every word of this book and kept true
to my voice and my grammatical quirks;

To Alexander Orion Sparks who wrestled with
the concepts of every article to create its best image;

To all my best girlfriends, too numerable to name,
who have taught me the deeply satisfying joy
of their sweet, unconditional love;

To my brothers for modeling how to be respectful,
loving, and kind to their wives and children for over 30 years;

To my mother who taught me outward confidence
and a love for language;

To my father who taught me the life-saving journey
of the 12 steps of AA;

To Patrick Sparks for being an impeccable father to our son
and for revealing an education
that gave space for him to become a human being.

Finally to my son, Alexander,
for his integrity, brilliance, and open-heartedness.
He dared me to write this book.
Thank you. TaDaa!

Foreword

Penni Sparks shares her years of wisdom throughout these beautiful pages. She is an inspirational light who shares her experience, strength, and hope from years of dedication to her own inner work.

Penni will lead you on a transformational journey through the alphabet with practical tools for everyday life. Her intuitive gifts will assist you in your daily interactions and inspire you to reflect on your own behavior instead of others. This reflection assists in living in harmony versus using survival or defensive tactics that no longer are serving.

This book comes to us in divine timing for humanity!

Instead of feeling powerless, you will be inspired to shine as your authentic self!

Brigitte Parvin
Author of *How to Get Your Life Back*

Preface

When humans speak, I see what they are saying.

By that I do not simply mean I understand what they're saying; I literally 'see' what they're saying. Images arise (sometimes even movies!) directly connected to their spoken words, and I wonder if they are aware of what their words look like.

So I ask, "Did you hear what you just said?"

Humans can solve their own problems with the words they choose to describe them, however sometimes they haven't yet consciously strengthened their intuitive organs of perception to hear what they're saying to themselves.

As an enthusiastic linguistics nerd, I see the roots and secret power words hold. I see new ways to approach situations by changing the dialogue or playing a word-game.

That's how my mind has played with me for as long as I can remember, and I have, over the years, shared these games with friends and colleagues. In August 2019, my son dared me to post one of my games on Instagram, which I have done (and some) over the course of the year.

Now, from the core of my being, I offer the basics of my inner-games, my ABC's of Being Human in book form. I hope it serves as a how-to guide to reach for when you find yourself stuck in a situation that turns your insides out.

I offer no guarantees except that if you keep an open mind, these games will not harm you, nor will they encourage you to harm anyone else. They simply offer a new way to look into the world, a new way to receive the world, and a new way to communicate both with the world and with yourself.

With gratitude, I'm serving up this bowl of alphabet soup of basic inner-games that help me be kind when interacting with other human beings.

I hope it feeds you to the core of your being!

Penni Sparks

Kona, HI

August 2020

Table of Contents

Appreciations

Foreword by Brigitte Parvin

Preface

I

is for

Imagine

Imagine you are standing on a stage in an auditorium filled with 500 people who know you. The MC asks everyone who loves you to stand up. 499 people stand up. Isn't that amazing? What do you see? Many, if not most of us, would focus on the ONE.

Welcome to my inner mind and heart and allow me to introduce you to my Old Belief System. In this scenario, my mind starts attacking me:

"What did I ever do to you? Are you disappointed in me, jealous of me, or assuming lies about me?"

Such thoughts ring so loudly that I only contemplate:

"How can I get back at her?"
"How can I make him say he's sorry to me?"
"How can I change what just happened?"

These rants rarely give room for reason, such as:

"Are you physically unable to stand?"
"Are you in the wrong auditorium?"
"Do you actually have a legitimate beef with me?"

I am left standing on the stage, frozen in false fear, believing I'm unwanted, unloved, and alone. Meanwhile, I completely disregard the 499 friends standing there who have said they love me.

Does this sound familiar? My thoughts not only try to convince me of a point of view not grounded in truth, they try to avert my eyes from the overwhelming love that is present in the room.

This habitual way of thinking leaves me in a state of ignorance. That is, it leads me to 'ignore' the entire picture and choose only to zoom in on 1/500th of reality. What an unbalanced perception!

Today I have a New Belief System. Now, I strive to be awake and aware of the whole picture and I am filled with gratitude for all that IS. I believe there is a Stream of Fearlessness that is available to everyone, and I choose to flow within that stream. I actively look for and acknowledge the abundance of beauty, truth, and goodness that decorate every day.

I've come to understand that out of all that happens, very few challenges arise that are my responsibility to solve on my own. There is a bounty of gifts that await each of us when we choose to look for them. My days are filled with unexpected synchronicities of grace and guidance and blessings beyond measure that allow me to hear the inspired solutions for myself and those around me.

This New Belief System is no fairytale; I believe it's our birthright — yours and mine, as human beings, and I want to remind you of it.

So with gratitude and newfound courage, I offer *The ABC's of Being Human*. I offer an alphabet soup, not necessarily alphabetically, representing games of inner work that you can play to help you remember who you are, to help you bless those who are in ignorance, and to help you choose to thrive in the Stream of Fearlessness buoyed by the many who love you.

So enjoy, Dear Friends!

And please share this with your 499.

A is for Awake

There are so many acceptable ways to be asleep these days — through substances, pills, programs, work, technologies, processed foods, radical or exclusive belief systems, hatred, shaming, blaming, passivity, judgment, gossip, lazy vocabulary, being small, and not liking things, to name a few.

One of the first spiritual books I read as a young adult described the world as the top of an iceberg surrounded by water. Every square inch of the land was populated by all the usual, unconscious interactions human beings have with calamities, unkindnesses, fears, and chaotic encounters, each attempting to make us choose to PAY our attention to it.

Then suddenly, without expecting it, one human being stumbles across a DOOR in the ground and opens it to discover the breadth of the ocean below — a vast expanse of calm and peace; of flow and generosity and time and space; of creativity and passion and wonder and awe and inclusivity and kindness and joy and gratitude.

To PAY attention is a curious phrase, isn't it? The power of the words assumes our attention is quite the commodity of trade in the world, something of great value, not only to us, but to others as well.

What are you getting for your attention? Are you making a conscious choice about how to SPEND it, or are you simply 'following the market trend' and spending it however those around you are spending it?

I hope to be choosing to pay MY attention quite consciously to how I drive, how I interact with others, what I do with my trash, what foods I eat, what magazines I read, what shows I watch, what conversations I engage in, what jokes I tell, and what words I use to express myself.

Especially when surrounded by the bustle of the world, I strive to be AWAKE to the abundant treasure of my cherished values awaiting me behind the DOOR that I open when I PAY attention. When I do, I receive gifts of grace from the Prosperity of Spirit, from the Breath of Goodness and Love that continues to multiply to support and protect human beings, no matter what we're walking through.

How AWAKE do YOU want to be?

B is for Busy

Are your days so very full from your first breath in the morning until your final, fleeting thought at night that the most common word you use throughout the day to describe yourself is 'BUSY?'

I was a single mom and a full-time educator, a part-time consultant, a mostly-present girlfriend, and a budding author, while shooting a pilot for a TV show on parenting. At the height of what I fondly call my 'Busy Period', I used that word as a one-size-fits-all response to describe why I just didn't have a few minutes for you or your concerns or to join your cause or go to lunch or to chat with you after a meeting. I thought I had no choice but to be busy!

I was so convinced that 'busy' was an admirable quality, I decided to travel to the Bay Area on the weekend and seek out a Chinese calligrapher for a rainbow rendition of the word to frame for my office. Once I found a street artisan whose aesthetic pleased me, I made my request and waited and watched as the gentle flow of the characters covered the canvas.

Now I do not speak Chinese, however I do know that it is a language different from ours in that our words use letters, while their words use individual glyphs or pictures that each have meaning. So as he worked, I started asking questions about the glyphs he was painting.

"What does that first glyph stand for?" I asked excitedly, because I just knew this was going to be really supportive and inspirational — a word I could be deeply proud to use to describe myself.

"Heart. It means heart," he said quietly. Of course it meant heart! Heart is good — this was going to be even better than I imagined.

"So what does the second glyph mean?" I asked, now even more excited to hear what kind of heart I had or how big and loving it was.

"Second character is killing — no, MURDERING."

Busy is Heart Murdering.

I quietly paid him and thanked him for his artistry. I drove home and put it on my wall in a place where I could make certain to look at it every day.

It's been 15 years since, and to the best of my ability, I have ceased using that word to describe myself or anyone else. I even stop friends who use the word and tell them this story, in case they, too, would care to stop using it.

Think about it. To lump all the day's opportunities, encounters, and gifts received into a generic pile labeled 'BUSY' desperately misrepresents the fullness of life. It is a dishonorable label to say the least.

Instead, I say that my day is full or that I live a life so blessed beyond measure that I have no room left for anything more right now. I was once told that a sign of maturity is saying 'No' to something you want to do, but cannot for whatever reason.

Today my plate is full of the people and activities I've chosen to fill it. I easily decline when offered an opportunity I have no room for or have no desire for, just as I would respond if someone offered me organic boiled okra at a potluck.

"No, thank you, and thanks for inviting me."

Grace made it possible for me to survive my 'B Period,' and I remain forever grateful to those angelic human beings who supported me and my heart when I thought I needed to do and be it

9

all. Now I consciously choose words to reflect how grateful I am for the myriad opportunities that have come my way, and I say 'Yes' only when I mean it and have space for it.

By the way, my Chinese calligraphy still hangs prominently in my office, and my heart is full and in perfect health.

C
is for
COWs

I've discovered a way to stop being the unwilling victim of my own skewed perception. It's quite simple — I avoid COWs!

Imagine a vast meadow of wildflowers so abundant that you cannot take a step without crushing one — I've seen such a vision in Wyoming. Somewhere in that bucolic field are also fresh cow pies.

A natural question might be, "Where did that s**t come from?" In a field of wildflowers, of course, it comes from ruminating cows. Now, consider a similar landscape as an image of our thought-lives.

I KNOW I have the ability to fill my mind with abundant, creative, and colorful ideas, memories, and wonderings. Then every so often, somebody does something or says something or doesn't say or do something that RUINS everything, leaving me with a pile of mind-manure.

This also comes from COWs, however not the adorable Jersey or impressive Texas Longhorn varieties. 'COWs' is a TLA (three letter acronym) for soul habits we unconsciously allow to muck up the lush, verdant possibilities of our thinking.

Unconscious Soul Habit #1 is Conditions

I'm a believer in unconditional love, yet I find I'm not a perfect practitioner of it. My mind creates conditions for love and acceptance more often than I would care to admit.

> "If you really loved me, you'd know exactly what I want for my birthday."
> "If he were mature, he wouldn't speak to me like that."
> "If she were responsible, she'd know not to do that."
> "If you were a friend, you would never treat me this way."

When Conditions are present, Love is not. When I let go of Conditions, I can then notice the abundant supply of Love that is a around me and it is MINE for the taking! I get to marvel at how many ways there are to be human.

Unconscious Soul Habit #2 is Outcomes

When I hold on to the expectation of a certain outcome, I limit the possible solutions to only that one scenario.

> "Once I get my promotion, people will start listening to me."
> "Once I'm a size 8, I'll find my true love."
> "Once she's out of the house, everything will be ok."
> "As soon as he gets a degree, I'll go to coffee with him."

When Outcomes are present, Grace is absent. When I let go of Outcomes, I allow my life to be filled with what the Infinite Power of the Universe has planned for me.

Unconscious Soul Habit #3 is War

When I hear myself using war-like vocabulary, I know I'm mentally getting ready for battle. I start taking stock of how much wrong-doing is on your side and how much right-doing is on my side. I look for self-righteous justification for character assassination (gossip), undercutting your reputation, or knocking the legs out from under the other guy, just to make certain I look good.

> "I'm going to set a boundary."
> "I've got a good come-back for that."
> "I'm on her side!"
> "Whose fault is it?"

War, on any level, is not how I wish to spend my energy.

When War is being plotted, Peace cannot abide. When I let go of War, the ways of Peace arise as new inspiration for all of us to be heard and for each of us to get our needs met.

Whenever I feel agitated, I start looking for COWs: Conditions, Outcomes, and War. Where am I setting Conditions on the behavior of others? What Outcome am I convinced is the ONLY one worth considering? How am I attempting to set up an army of followers ready to 'be on my side' when the War begins?

Once I realize that I can step away from the COWs and be present in the field, I find there is no longer any wrong-doing or right-doing — just as Rumi told us long ago.

> "Out beyond the ideas of wrong-doing and right-doing there is a field; I'll meet you there."

M is for Magnet

Think back to 6th grade physics class when the teacher asked the question, "What does a magnet do?" I'll bet you answered: "It attracts or repels," which, of course, we all know, right?

Guess what, even though your teacher smiled and said you were right, you actually weren't!

Yes, we've all seen one magnet bond to another magnet, and we've all seen two magnets refuse to touch. However, in either case, were the magnets intentionally, actively attracting or repelling?

Imagine yourself as a magnet, just being at home or being at work, and you're fully charged. Suddenly, some other magnets approach. Depending on your charge and their charges, those magnets might come into your space or they might quickly move away.

Are you, as a magnet, really doing something to have power over those magnets, to attract or to repel them? What's really going on here?

Is one magnet attracting another? If so, how do you know which of the two is doing the attracting? If all magnets have the ability to attract, why are some repelling? Are we asking the right questions? What if this scenario has nothing to do with attraction?

Each magnet has its charge, its own being-ness, and depending on what the charge is, it will be of interest or not of interest to those magnet-beings who pass by. Its being-ness will not, however, have power over them.

True being-ness has no conditions on the behavior of those who pass by; it has no hope for a certain outcome to strengthen the quality of its own being-ness; it has no opposition to those around it or a need to convert or sway other magnets to hold a charge that is attractive to its own being-ness. It's just self-contained, self-assured, clear, consistent, and just being itself — a magnet.

Since we're imagining ourselves to be magnets, we all get to share those qualities of being-ness, too. We all get to be who we truly are at our core. We all get to play for fun and for free.

Interestingly enough, the word 'magnet' also has nothing to do with attraction; it simply identifies the place in Greece where the first such rock with unique powers, magnetite, was found — in Magnesia. But that's another story...

So back to the original question, "What do magnets do?"

In scientific terms magnets display. They are who they are, and they freely, unconditionally display. It's the rest of the environment that chooses to act in relationship to the magnet or not; the magnet, however, simply displays.

What do you display? Do you keep your true charge no matter who walks by? Are you aware of who you truly are at your core? Are you able to retain your display regardless of what other magnets around you are doing, feeling, thinking, and saying?

By choosing to practice the Way of a Magnet, I'm no longer to blame for the energy disruptions of the people around me, nor do I need to waste my energy trying to attract them to what I'm doing, feeling, thinking, or saying. No one around me has to change so that my world is better. I operate my own human climate controls, and I attempt to keep my environment consistent, encouraging, welcoming, and safe.

I can be at peace with and in quiet acceptance of who I am, and I can display myself accordingly. I can remind myself that I can choose to be stimulated by what other magnets do or not do. I can patiently wait for what is attracted to my natural being-ness, my display, rather than actively attempting to make others be what I want them to be.

For example, I can choose to display serenity. Isn't it interesting to know that the root of the word serenity is 'serene,' which, in other parts of the world, is a title of high nobility, as in "Her Most Serene Highness."

So today I choose to be a magnet of serenity; I put on my inner crown and most serenely display who I truly am, no matter what.

What do you choose to display?

N

is for

New Moon

From the study of astronomy over the last several decades, I've marveled at the accuracy of ancient accountings from naked-eye observations and how they demonstrate the extraordinary relationship astronomers had with the stars that is not as present or possible today. I've come to wonder if the stars once spoke to human beings and if humans could hear them and speak back.

The period of the three days of the New Moon, when the moon seems to disappear from the night sky then reappear as a mere sliver, was a mysterious and magical time in ancient cultures.

Stories prevail among almost every indigenous people to explain this monthly phenomenon. One of my favorites is from Ancient Egyptian culture.

For the Egyptians, the Sun was a powerful, omnipresent god for whom they had many names, Ra being one. They actually had distinct names for the sun at each place it stood during the course of the day. The people knew not to speak directly with a power that burned their eyes just to look upon it, so they had to create a different way to speak with Ra.

During the night, the people learned to work with the Moon whose light and presence was soothing and welcoming. They hope the Moon would be better able to carry their concerns to Ra. The people noticed the slow disappearance of the monthly Moon and its reappearance as a fingernail sliver in the sky, which for them became an empty cup, an empty hand.

Into this chalice they placed their questions, concerns, and cares.

Over the weeks that followed, the New Moon gradually waxed more full of light with each night's viewing. The people watched, knowing the light of their god, the Sun, was gradually filling this empty chalice with enlightened answers, guidance, and loving care.

When the Full Moon rose two weeks later, the people had their answers. Then, they could bask in the Light of the care and insight of a power greater than themselves. When the next New Moon came, they were prepared with their next question, ready to place it into the Silver Sliver for the spiritual world to answer.

I find there is so much timeless wisdom from the study of the practices of ancient cultures. Their simple reliance on the ever-present working of the spiritual world at the mere request of a human being is probably the most unpracticed cure for what ails humanity today.

Imagine creating a life where you naturally rely on a power greater than yourself, whatever name you give it, to offer you the care and guidance you need, and all you have to do is simply ask for it!

What question or concern have you been meaning to place into the care of the open, loving hand of a power greater than you? Are you willing to quietly wait for two weeks for answers to be gradually revealed to you?

When is the next New Moon?

H
is for
Huli

My home is a shrine to my friends. Pretty much everywhere you look, there is something a dear one has painted, sculpted, written, crafted, purchased, photographed, or woven for me. In this way I'm always surrounded by loved ones, and almost everything has a story that plays in my heart when I look at it.

Recently, a friend gifted me with a beautifully hand-turned, cherrywood bowl he had crafted, and it reminds me of one of my favorite ancient Hawaiian tales of Ho'oponopono.

When the news of a woman, a 'wahine,' being pregnant is announced, an elder, a 'kapuna,' begins to carve a bowl from a carefully chosen piece of wood. As the kapuna works, thoughts of how each unique human being is mindfully carved by the Wise One imbue this earnest work.

The bowl is presented to the mother on the event of the birth, and it holds the light of the being who is newly born. The child, and bowl, become vessels for the essence, the 'mana', of who the child truly is.

As the young one grows more independent, challenges arise and difficult interactions occur that make the child unconsciously pick up a pebble, a 'pohaku' of a belittling belief or a recurring resentment, thinking it is hers to keep. Each time she feels ill-at-ease, angry, fearful, doubtful, unworthy, shameful, or inadequate, another pohaku is added to her bowl, and each time, the pohaku displaces some of her light.

Fortunately, she has been taught to 'huli' her bowl every night before she goes to bed. When she remembers this priceless practice of turning the bowl upside-down to empty out all the pohaku, all that is not her true essence, she sleeps in peace, knowing who she truly is.

Sometimes, there are days when she forgets to huli her bowl, and then she feels less and less her whole self. Once she remembers, though, no matter the time of day, she can mindfully huli her bowl and rid herself of her dis-ease.

You too, have been carved by the Master's Hand and filled with the light essence of who you truly are.

Have you remembered to huli your bowl today?

Q
is for
Quiver

In my 20s, before the days of cell phones and YouTube, I listened to late-night radio talk shows for entertainment and vital information about life. At that point in my own life, not yet having received a single marriage proposal and feeling like a failure, I particularly enjoyed the radio talk shows about how to find a loving relationship.

On one particular evening, the topic was "What is the secret to your long-term marriage?" I listened for all kinds of answers, so that if anyone ever did ask me to marry them, I would know how to make it last forever. Here is one story I remember.

The couple being interviewed said that initially, whenever a mood or a situation entered their home that made either of them feel uncomfortable or unsafe or unloved, by default they would reach for their 'quiver of verbal arrows' and turn to take aim at the other.

> "You brought this mess into our home!"
>
> "No, you brought it when you said what you said!"
>
> "I never said anything like that. You're too sensitive."
>
> "You seem to have a problem with acceptance."
>
> "It's always all about you, isn't it?!"

Sound familiar?

For years this was their way of addressing disagreements. They automatically assumed the other was the problem and aimed an arrow accordingly. One day one of them realized they could do something different with their bows and arrows.

They got a large bowl from the kitchen cabinet and put it on the coffee table in the living room, where most of their arguments began. The next time a challenge arose, one of them said:

> "A Big Problem has just entered the room. Can you feel how it's making us take sides? It's about to divide us

for the rest of the evening. I'm going to gather it up and place it in this bowl."

"Let's sit, side-by-side, and aim our arrows at the true invader. Instead of tearing each other down by aiming our arrows of blame, shame, and guilt at one another, we can combine our creative, loving power to take aim at the PROBLEM!"

How many arguments could be avoided by seeking a solution together rather than focusing on whom to blame for the problem?

Imagine a world full of Agents of Change, human beings whose well-armed quivers are filled with arrows of curiosity, creative solutions, open-mindedness, generosity, and willingness.

Pausing when agitated provides an opportunity to choose from this quiver instead. In those moments, when a new perspective or a new approach comes to me, I'm filled with awe, relief, joy, and a visceral sense of the ever-present working of the spiritual world!

I wish the same experience for each of you this week, just once. Keep your quiver close! After that, I hope you'll get hooked on the practice as I have!

S
is for
Spiritual
Food Groups

Years ago I discovered a surprising key to losing weight. I ha~
erroneously thought that eliminating fats from my daily intake woul~
yield a quicker weight loss. To my surprise, only when I prepared
balanced meals made up of foods from all the food groups,
including fats, did I achieve a nourished, healthy, balanced body.

So I wondered, if that's true in the physical world, it must als~
be true in the spiritual world. What spiritually nourishing food
groups, then, must I partake of on a daily basis to maintain a
healthy, balanced spirit?

Here are My Four Spiritual Food Groups:

Connect to Your Spiritual Source

Whatever that means to you, whether it's a physical or devotional practice; prayers and verses; attending services; singing; journaling; painting; dancing; connect daily to the Spiritual Source that is your constant companion, your source of light and purpose and joy. This one practice is the staff of a balanced life!

Take Care of Your Personal Needs

Whatever your personal responsibilities are for the day, do them. By that I mean brush your teeth; pay your bills; get to appointments on time; return phone calls (if only to say you need to reschedule for another day); dress appropriately; feed yourself nourishing food and drink plenty of water; maintain your living space, your car, and your yard; and mind your manners.

Be of Anonymous Service

Pick up trash that you see; be kind to a person in retail or customer service; donate blood or clothing or food; put your phone away when you're walking so you can say 'hello' to whomever you encounter; be awake enough to open doors for others – men, women, old, young – and say 'thank you' when they do the same for you.

There are so many ways to be of service to others; however, this is a little different. It's anonymous. When carried out without letting anyone know what you're doing, service is a nourishing practice for you while helping the people you serve.

Play

This was the surprising one to me, like the role of 'fats' in the world of nutrition.

When I had my son, I fed him well, helped him make chore charts, and kept a clean house; however, I had no idea how to play with him. I didn't experience a very playful childhood myself. I felt like someone was watching me and keeping a scorecard, and I only got points for working hard. Period. This was one old belief I did not wish to pass along to my child.

One day I made the conscious choice to sit outside with my son in the dirt with his buckets of water and cars and sticks, to watch what he was doing, and to follow his lead. After that day, I let him teach me to swing high, to tell stories and to make movies, to paint, and to read beautiful, meaningful books.

Now, I love to sing, to be with my friends, to snorkel, to travel, to work puzzles, to Zumba!, to watch vintage TV shows, and to shop thrift stores. I do at least one of these every day.

What do you do for fun?

Growing up, I never once used the word 'kale' in a sentence, and now I eat it almost everyday. I've also moved from Crisco to coconut oil and from ice cream to frozen berries. My physical habits are so much more conscious now that I've become aware of how important it is for me to choose to be an active participant in my own health.

Are you nourishing your spiritual life as rigorously as you nourish your physical body?

Are you an active participant in the development of your spiritual health?

The Latin root, 'sanos,' means health or balance, and it is the root of the word 'sanity.' Is your life sane, or is it a little in-sane, a little out of balance?

Which of the Spiritual Food Groups could you have a little more of? A little less of?

Today, I've replaced my childhood prayers with inspirational words that touch my soul deeply, and I say vintage verses that bring me to tears with their power. Remembering to feed myself just the right words at just the right moment reminds me who I am and why I'm here.

I'm more conscious than ever when I'm in the nourishing presence of the Power of Love, on all levels.

N
is for
No
Trespassing

A well-known Aramaic prayer was borrowed by one religion, adopted by another, and is widely spoken today. Even though it has been translated into a multitude of languages and adopted by a myriad of cultures, one of its messages is still NOT a best practice among human beings.

This line refers to a lingering human habit:

"Forgive us our trespasses, as we forgive those who trespass against us."

Apparently, human beings have been trespassing for hundreds of generations, and we still haven't learned that it's not the best use of our free will.

Why is it that we think it's our task to step into other people lives, especially when we haven't been invited? I know I feel uncomfortable, even violated, when someone steps into my life, uninvited, answers a question I haven't asked or offers unsolicited advice. Oddly, I'm often left with a feeling that I should be thanking them... for an intrusion.

The following declarations contain no 'calls to action,' and yet are commonly misunderstood as invitations to trespass; considered more closely, they are merely statements.

> "I just don't know what to do."
> "I'm so lost."
> "I'm scared and I feel so alone."
> "I'll never figure out how to do this."

Too often such words are followed by suggestions, rebuttal or directions, as if the speaker had made a request, rather than a statement.

Instead of barging straight in, try stopping at someone's gat and asking permission to enter their yard, their life. Such a pause offers them the dignity to ask for advice, support, or help, if they want any.

A more welcomed response might be:

"I'm listening. Is there more?"
"How may I help?"
"I'm right here."
"Please, let me know what you need."
"Would you like some suggestions?"

Responding with a statement of unconditional support or a follow-up question is often more helpful than the 'help' of an uninvited opinion. It also gives the other a chance to say:

"Thank you for your concern, for your care."
"Thank you for being here."
"Thank you for asking. I'll let you know."
"Thank you."

Inviting someone specifically to ask for the help they need gives them the unexpected gift of feeling the dignity of being more in control of a seemingly hopeless situation. It's certainly more helpful than contributing to the myth that, without your input, they are incapable or ignorant of the next right thing to do.

From another perspective, consider the words, "I just don't know what to do." They don't ask directly for help or for any call to action. They dangle a passively unclear statement and wait to see who takes the bait and tries to correctly 'guess' the unspoken need. Too often the one attempting to help is labeled inept or unloving, when they're simply not good at mind-reading.

Beware of the words, "I don't know what to do." They are NOT public domain; they are a temptation to trespass!

Just think of the peaceful healings that could infect the world if we chose to finally heed that one ancient suggestion.

Here's an attempt at a new translation:

"Forgive me for stepping into the lives of others,
when I haven't been invited,
as I forgive those who step into my life,
when I haven't invited them."

I invite you to practice NO TRESPASSING. Try to wait serenely at the gate to be invited into the lives of others.

And remember to be patient and to forgive those who, without being invited, trespass into your life.

P

is for

Peace

All I've ever wanted was Peace.

As a young girl I watched The Ed Sullivan Show on TV every
December, patiently waiting, cross-legged on the floor, for the
global children's choir to sing, "Let There be Peace on Earth." I
remember the hopeful joy on the face of every small being, dressed
in uniquely individual clothes with hair styles, skin tones, and eye
shapes I had rarely ever seen.

Later on, as a choir director, my uniquely individual choirs sang it, too, with the same simple, unadorned unison of the children's choir my heart remembered.

I've enjoyed many professions: Judo instructor; 5-star French restaurant manager; early morning radio DJ; small business consultant; parenting coach; youth group facilitator; survival canoeist; inspirational workshop leader; teachers' teacher; high school director; and K-12 educator.

A seemingly disconnected collection of professions, no doubt, yet whenever asked why I do what I do, the answer has always been the same: I guide human beings away from entering into war over situations, relationships, or decisions.

More accurately, I remind human beings to CHOOSE PEACE.

I was attracted to the ideas of an Austrian philosopher who came forward at the end of WWI with the idea that educating our children in a new way could put forth the seeds for social renewal, so that human beings would never need to enter into a world war again.

Although his plan for peace was not adopted by world leaders at the time, his curriculum and indications for educating our youth has lived a rich, 100-year span of time, enriching the lives of developing human beings with a sense of worldwide inclusivity, an appreciation for the beauty, truth, and goodness of all that is, and a desire to contribute back to humanity through what they love most. And every human being gets a seat at the table, in Peace.

As a human being, how do I choose peace in a world where war at every level is so prevalent?

In the presence of Free Will, where I am free to do whatever I want for whatever reason I want, why choose peace?

Exactly!

As you've already noticed, some don't choose peace.

Sometimes war can be so temporarily fulfilling!

A plethora of supposedly empowering emotions and endorphins are released with 'knowing I'm right and you're wrong'; with 'choosing the perfect, humiliating words to slay someone who's wronged me'; or with 'gathering an army of like-minded soldiers ready to do battle with whatever issue comes along.' All for the sheer sake of winning!

What happens if I allow the warmongering to pass and I WAIT, and I CHOOSE PEACE instead?

WAIT is an acronym for: Why Am I Talking?

What if the first step in choosing peace is to pause before saying anything?

What if the next step in choosing peace is to conquer the inner battles trying to convince me I have the RIGHT to War?

If I indeed have the RIGHT to War, I also have the RIGHT to Choose Peace, and all I have to do is WAIT.

What do I do while I'm WAIT-ing?

WAIT-ing for the war in my head to stop?

WAIT-ing for the voices of the armies to stop seeming so attractive?

WAIT-ing for the choice for Peace to arise within my soul?

I play Soul Games that allow me to practice the daily habit of Choosing Peace, while WAIT-ing in these inner and outer War Zones.

Please allow me to introduce them to you.

Peace Games

T

is for

Three Seconds

Peace Game #1

Pausing in silence has never worked for me; my mind is simply too active to just calm down because I have asked it to. So I create games to keep it occupied, while I attempt to consciously adjust my breathing, keep my mouth shut, and pray that this works before I accidentally get myself into trouble again.

Some days I'm just powerless over my thoughts, my reactions, and especially over judgments of myself, of others, and of the world. I feel hopeless that it will always be this way, no matter how many books I read, no matter how many candles I light, no matter how many classes I take, no matter what.

I feel like there's a war going on inside my head, between me and my hopes for another outcome.

How can I hope for Peace without when there's barely Peace within?

When no one else is around, my own thoughts can be negative, judgmental, accusatory, self-deprecating, shaming, blaming, and guilt-ridden. I speak about myself TO myself in ways I would hope never, ever to speak about or to anyone else.

Yet that habitual, unconscious, default inner-speech festers and seeps out to attack others when I'm not on my best guard. I always regret it and need to make amends for my automatic, thoughtless unkindnesses.

What would it take to bring Peace to my mind... to end these reactive, warlike, default thoughts?

The first step toward Peace is to recognize that War is present, and that begins right here in my own body, in my own mind.

My body often knows before I do when the option for War has entered my life. I notice various physical changes almost immediately: my heart rate increases, my teeth clench, my brow wrinkles, my eyes roll or focus-in on my 'target,' my breathing changes, my muscles tense, and I want to leave or hit something.

At the same time, my brain is leading the charge, reminding me I have the Right to War, giving me permission to express exaggerated emotions, witty comebacks, and sarcastic remarks, so I'll either win or at least be funny.

Interestingly, if you look at the root of the word 'sarcasm,' it's not funny at all. 'Sarkos' is a Greek word meaning 'to strip off the flesh,' and isn't that just what it feels like when something sarcastic is said or heard?

Years ago a mentor of mine gave me a gift that changed my life. She held out her hand and asked me to hold out mine. As she opened hers, she placed Three Seconds into my hand and challenged me to use them to pause time and give witness to a situation before I chose to say or do anything.

With those Three Seconds, I was given the opportunity to detach momentarily before I reacted in the same old way. Physically, in my brain, I also began the long process of detaching from the default, familiar, habitual synaptic paths that made me say and do things that felt out of my control.

Sometimes I still feel like I'm being forced into the ruts of saying what I've always said and doing what I've always done. My default reactions are 'brain ruts,' and it takes conscious, willing road repair to fill in those ruts and find another path for my thinking to follow.

So now that I could pause TIME for Three Seconds, I also needed to pause SPACE.

I needed to separate myself from any situation and become an objective observer of my life. I needed a new perspective for old situations, so a new voice might arise to guide me along new pathways of being with myself, with others, and with the world.

I needed a new auto-response that didn't hurt anyone, myself included, that didn't put anyone in a box with a label, that didn't divide me from others, and did not lead me into War.

So I added three words to those Three Seconds — "Isn't that interesting?"

These magical words are one-size-fits-all when it comes to what my mind encounters in the world. Whether it's when someone cuts me off in traffic; or when someone dismisses me in a discussion or when someone fails to say please or thank you; or even when someone merely wears an odd print or orders weird food, I say to myself:

> "Isn't that interesting? I really want to judge her."
> "Isn't that interesting? I really want to say something witty and unkind just to get back at him."
> "Isn't that interesting? I just called myself 'stupid' for a human error."

"Isn't that interesting? I really want to correct what she just said."

"Isn't that interesting? I really think I am stupid, less than, or not worth the effort."

Mind you, I only say "Isn't that interesting?" to myself, not out loud to anyone else! I'm not looking for a new outer response; I'm practicing speaking more kindly to myself first.

I'm attempting to notice how much road repair my thought-ruts need. No one needs to know about my new habit of peaceful thinking. If I suddenly burst into laughter, and someone asks me what's going on, I let them know I'm practicing a new form of inner work and let it go.

Funny thing is, as I practice this new tack, I find life is naturally more delightful and calm. I often smile while noticing how I was just about to toss in a perfectly good day in exchange for War with someone with a different opinion or questionable driving habits or an inefficient solution or an unstylish jacket or poor grammar or an inconvenient food plan or a fervent religious or political idea different from my own.

The Right to War is cunning, baffling, and powerful, and as I pause for Three Seconds to notice how unimportant my unconscious reaction to all of it is, I find Peace has a greater chance to repair the damage War has done to my thought-life over the years.

So please open your hand to receive Three Seconds, along with the inner practice to say to yourself, no matter what happens, "Isn't that interesting?"

Peace Game:

D

is for

Defuse

Peace Game #2

As a teacher, a mother, an employer, a colleague, a partner, a daughter, a sibling, a student, a leader, and a friend, I have experienced a lifetime of tense situations that, at any moment, could have escalated into War. When those situations arise, I never know when I, or the other may be 'in the mood' to misunderstand, to take offense, to blame, assume, misinterpret, or to choose NOT to presume goodwill.

This 'Mood' of the possibility of War can sometimes be attributed to being

too Hungry,

too Angry,

too Lonely,

too Tired.

My son and I call this being HALT-ed, and we have used the awareness of this possible 'mood' to pause a heated conversation until one or both of us can take care of whatever part of HALT needs attention. We have defused many potentially explosive situations with this simple game of HALT.

It's easy to defuse a situation when both parties are consciously committed to Peace. However, what happens when a random conversation becomes suddenly tense because one person throws in some words or a message or an email or a text that lands like an attack, a Social Bomb?

How do I defuse this possible escalation into War before the bomb goes off and destroys a relationship, a reputation, or a future possibility of peaceful interaction?

The more I know about Social Bombs, the more successfully can defuse them. So here's what I've come to know about tricky communication.

Human beings love to be appreciated, love to be heard, and love to be right — right?! So I've employed these common attributes to lead me into a 3-Step Plan to Defusing Social Bombs.

Step One: "Thank You"

The two most powerful, one-size-fits-all words for any situation are 'thank you.'

No matter what I encounter, whenever I can begin a response with an authentic 'thank-you,' the impending doom of possible War almost immediately defuses.

> "Thank you for taking the time to let me know about this challenging situation."
>
> "Thank you for having the courage to call me and bring this to my attention."
>
> "Thank you for so clearly sharing your experience of this difficulty."
>
> "Thank you for your passion regarding your child's needs."

Step Two: "Pardon Me For…"

The next most powerful words are, "Pardon me for not being clear."

Often, I find, I am not always entirely clear when communicating. I may think I was clear, however, if there is a miscommunication, or in some way a lack of clarity was present, and I'm willing to take full responsibility for the lack of clarity, we can move more quickly toward defusing the situation.

These words can leave the other person with a sense of NOT BEING WRONG, and that's pretty close to being right — right?!

I find these words are a small price to pay for allowing the other person to know I'm safe and that I'm not going to argue about who's right and who's wrong. I am simply interested in clearing up the misunderstanding and keeping Peace.

Step 3: "Is There More?"

At this point my only job is to LISTEN to whatever they have to say. If they say only a little, I encourage them to continue by asking, "Is there more?" I keep listening until they've said what they need to say.

I don't take what they say personally, and I don't respond or react.

This is important — this is where the explosion can happen: react to their reaction to my reaction and on and on…

Too often, hurt people hurt people, and if I'm willing to sit with others while they lance their own boil, drain their own wound, I'm more likely to find out they just needed to be heard, and we can move on.

When I remember to identify and defuse Social Bombs, I am less likely to suddenly erupt, blow-up in someone's face, blame someone for my own discomfort, my own dis-ease, or become irritable and unreasonable without knowing it.

I would never wish a Social Bomb on anyone, however if any come your way this week, I invite you practice defusing them with these three steps:

Thank you.
Pardon me for...
Is there more?

Peace Game #3

In my quiet contemplation this morning I had a vision. I saw a myriad of horizontal lines coming from all directions and focused or a center. The lines seemed dark and menacing, uninvited, accusing, and debilitating.

A column of light began to grow right in the center of it all, forming a simple human being in the midst of the light. She was the target of the attacks, yet she was peacefully safe in her column of light.

I have experienced such horizontal attacks. Sometimes it's merely blustery weather or an onslaught of traffic or blinding lights or harsh noises or too many people in a crowded area or neighborhood dogs barking all at once or a too-needy cat. All seem to attack my peace of mind.

Other times the horizontal attacks come as unwelcome words of judgment or humor at someone's expense... or dismissal of my contribution to a conversation or a cat-call or a put-down or rolling eyes.

Sometimes I don't need someone else to do the attacking. I attack myself with unreasonable, unkind expectations or self-criticisms.

My brain is especially practiced at two specific attacks.

The Arrogant, Intellectual Attack wants to convince me there is no need to ask for help; I can do this on my own. It makes me think that just one more Google search, one more self-help book or new-age label or exclusivity box will empower me to be the woman I was meant to be — self-sufficient and independent with all the right answers.

The Dogmatic, Moral Attack wants to take away my freedom of choice and turn me into an automaton who quotes others to justify my thoughts and opinions. Sadly, it promotes shame, blame, and guilt as the agreed upon results for not blindly following this path.

Each attack catches me off guard, and I'm left with thought of resentment and retaliation from feeling unsafe, ridiculed, alone, and disconnected.

Interestingly, the Latin word for reconnect, 'religare', is the root for our word 'religion.'

Standing freely amidst these attacks is an elevator available to take me away from the mess. It takes me to a state of feeling saf again, of feeling connected to something good that will protect and care for me.

This elevator is GRACE.

There is no way to earn entrance to the elevator, nor can I b denied it; there's nothing I have to do except to know that the elevator is there, step into it, and Go Vertical!

Grace is a warm, welcoming column of light that washes away the day, the moment, the attack, and you don't need a prescription for it!

When I'm feeling an attack brewing, I step to the right or the left of wherever I am, and I imagine I'm stepping into a column of light, into the elevator of Grace, and I Go Vertical!

When I Go Vertical, I feel reconnected to My Source and I'm safe. So, I invite you to Go Vertical, into Grace, into Peace.

R
is for
Red Ink Letters

My mind is often committed to taking me down. If I'm not actively awake, it keeps me harboring and rehashing resentments, seemingly failed relationships or interactions, and perceived past injuries, leaving me begging for restitution, revenge, or a stellar apology — at least in my imagination.

Those thoughts are viruses, pure venom, and they take up my energy, my health, and my balanced state of mind. I'm done being a host for such infections.

So I invented a practice called Red Ink Letters. All you need is paper, a red pen, and enough noisy anger in your head or heart that pretty much nothing else has a voice and nothing else can be heard.

Ready? Let's begin.

Light a candle to remind yourself that you have only one goal with any spiritual practice, and that is to connect cleanly, vertically with The Light of Love, The Source of All.

With this practice, the candle also serves as a visual reminder that the 'stuff' of this world is transformed by fire and air into Light. It also gives the momentary satisfaction of watching a situation go up in flames, but that's my 'red ink' talking. So my candle burns often to remind me I'm in the presence of the Unstoppable Transformation of Darkness.

Now, whatever is making you mad, whoever wounded you, whatever you're afraid you'll lose or never get, start writing it down in RED INK. You can start writing neatly in your best handwriting, but hopefully your anger will soon give you permission to scribble unrecognizably and carve so deeply into your paper that it makes an impression on the next page.

Lose the politically-correct language that we're all so trained to speak in, and start cussing like a sailor and give hell to whatever you're angry at — full force. The red ink and your red face are proof there's an infection, and we're doing some serious wound cleaning here!

Keep in mind that no one is going to read this except for you, so make sure you cover every tiny detail of every hurt, remove every little splinter. Don't hold back. Clean out your wound of all venom, pus, infection, dirt, filth, and anger.

All done? Then take a deep breath.

Now turn the pages over and grab a blue pen, a black pen, a pink pen, a sparkly gel pen, whatever pen delights your soul. Read through each anger-filled, putrefied phrase of your Red Ink Letter and see if you can find a hidden passion, flickering value, an unheard thank-you in it.

I often had the opportunity to play this game as a teacher. As an example, one day, after a full day of teaching and caring as completely as I was able for the welfare of 20+ students, I came home to a message from parents who sharply expressed their thorough disappointment in me because their child had come home with a half-eaten sandwich.

"Is it too much to ask for you to make certain he eats his whole lunch?"

As a single mom and a full-time teacher, I wanted so desperately to scream my frustration at this parent who obviously didn't have the whole picture. Instead, first I wrote my frustrations in a Red Ink Letter, and then, with the guidance of a loving colleague, slowly transformed each line into a common value, a shared passion or a thank-you.

Soon I had a response, a letter of gratitude that reflected the true me:

> "Thank you for having the courage to call me; I so appreciate direct speech when a problem arises. I share your passion for making certain that our children are well-nourished throughout the day, so they're ready to be their best. Do you have any ideas how we could bring this awareness to all the students in the class?
>
> "Thanks again for reaching out and please give my love to your child."

I started seeing every 'seeming attack' that came my way as an opportunity to transform it into a practice of seeing the whole picture and finding gratitude.

Hurt people hurt people. It became my primary purpose to identify our common values, so we were building up not tearing down in our work together for the children.

Today I continue to use this practice of Red Ink Letters to keep my energy clear of any harmful attacks, assumptions, and fears that try to divert me from using my energy for anything but loving kindness, no matter what.

Try a Red Ink Letter for yourself and feel free to contact me if you need help with the transformations. Sometimes the healing comes more readily when two or more are gathered.

A
Is for
Armor

Once again I'm awakened to the reality of how often, withou[t]
my knowing it, I'm in a state of preparing for War while thinking I'm a[ll]
about Peace.

Sometimes habitual word choices indicate preparation
strategies for an upcoming battle:

"Have you set a clear boundary with him?"
"What will you say if she says that again?"
"Whose side are you on?"

When I feel my teeth gritting for an uncomfortable encounter or my shoulders tightening to protect myself from whoever is coming through the door or over the phone, I know I have aligned myself with fear.

I've become pretty skilled at noticing such physical and psychological flags of fear's approach in my otherwise pretty peaceful life. I know the power of taking 3 deep breaths, or remembering to Go Vertical, or taking a Light Shower, and I can usually recover my own balance and health to meet the situation with calm confidence, kindness, and, at least outwardly, peace.

So now I'm digging deeper to find those unnoticeable ways that I've given my freewill over to fear without being conscious of my surrender.

When I was in college, I was a smoker. I was also a runner and a competitive judoka and, not having a car, I walked everywhere, up and down the hills of my Ohio University campus. So for me, the notion of smoking being a health risk (a rebellious thought held by many 'immortal' youth) was unfounded, even ridiculous, and my healthy, youthful body could prove it.

Then one day a spiritual mentor told me I was smoking to build up a protective ring of smoke around my heart, and as soon as I was certain I felt safe in the world, I would easily let go of smoking. The habit had become a form of 'armor.' As it turns out, the power of that image was enough to inspire me to do some inner work and indeed, the need to smoke was removed from me a short time later.

I've kept that powerful image with me and, over the years, have shared it with friends who were stuck and unable to stop smoking. They were grateful for a different perspective rather than struggling with the shame and guilt from loved ones meant as a means of inspiration to quit.

I wonder, how else am I putting on some kind of unconscious armor to protect myself?

Are there other reasons humans put on some form of self-armor as a means of self-care?

Do the words I use to describe myself have the power to design a protective shield that keeps me from fully living my life to my highest good for all concerned?

For a state of being to become armor, it would be chronic, developed over time. It would have to be common practice, a habit, as opposed to a one-time, appropriate response to a situation.

So what protections do these 'states of being' offer?

> Being overweight
> Being underweight
> Being shy
> Being sickly
> Being angry

Being judgmental

Being permissive

Being sad

Being uncomfortable with sadness

Being talkative

Being uncomfortable with silence

Being uncomfortable with differing opinions

What if each of these is an unconscious armor that, if the shackles could be located and unlocked, humans could be released from and be one step closer to inner peace?

If you had the chance learn how to unlock the binds, what self-armor would you choose to release?

S
is for
Stars

Who doesn't love stars?

My students simply loved to get stars, and I don't mean the younger ones. I mean my adolescents! I didn't give stars for correct answers or high scores. I played a game with them called Getting Caught in the Act of Doing Something Good (not doing something well!, so it was also a grammar game, but that's another article.)

Students would go about their day, and if I caught them clarifying an algebra problem during their recess time or helping someone pick up dropped papers or carrying a box for another teacher or opening a door for the person behind them, I would find them later and add a shiny, foil star to their 3x5 card that simply had their name on it.

Students could also catch someone else in the act of doing something good, tell me secretly, and I would add a shiny star to their friend's card.

Developing the new inner habit of watching out for the good others are doing, rather than watching out for what they're doing wrong, is a win/win for all human beings, isn't it?!

My thought was that the students could use these as collateral for a late or incomplete homework assignment. Weird thing is, they rarely wanted to use them for that — they wanted to keep their stars!

Now mind you, these stars had no other value. They didn't earn a pizza party or earn $1 for every 10. They were simply a record of being noticed for a free act of kindness, for doing something good.

When was the last time you got a star for the acts of kindness you sprinkle in the world throughout the day?

When was the last time you told someone you appreciate what you just witnessed them doing?

More importantly, do you give yourself a star

~ for remembering to eat how you want to eat?;

~ for completing a challenging task without complaining...
   much?;
~ for paying it forward in a long line?;
~ for not repeating a clever, unkind remark spoken at the
   expense of another?;
~ for choosing to be kind rather than clever?

I carry a small sheet of foil stars with me in my wallet. This week I handed one out to a busboy who was practicing 'social distancing' and safe service protocols throughout the restaurant, all with a smile on his face.

Another I handed to a woman who had just shared intimately in a group about how hard she'd been on herself until she awakened to her behavior, stopped speaking so harshly to herself, and made time for a massage.

Both people visibly lit up and smiled when I gave them stars.

I still have a paper weekly planner hanging on my refrigerator, mostly because I prefer foil stars to emoji stars.

As I walk by it, I remind my inner judge how many good things I've done today, and I smile. Someone's always watching; I know because I'm always watching, too, always judging myself!

Here are your first 10 gold stars, just because I already know about all the ways you've been thoughtful towards others and kind to yourself when you thought no one was watching.

Above all, let's be kind to one another, and to ourselves, during these interesting times.

Here are 5 extra credit stars, for staying open to this idea long enough to read this all the way to the end.

X
• is for •
eXpectations

Some days I look into the world and think, "If these people would stop doing that and those people would finally do this and those folks would stop saying such things and more people would start saying these things, we'd all be so much better."

When I string together too many of those days, where I'm just looking around to see what needs to change for me to feel better, I know an old friend has come to visit: eXpectations.

I've allowed my disappointment in you, in what you're not doing, or what you're doing the wrong way, to play as a tireless rerun. I know exactly what you need to change, if you'd only listen to me… or at least ask me!

Problem is, I've never been able to figure out how to get anyone to do what I want them to do. Even as a professional, when my success depended on someone else doing something 'right,' I usually failed.

To date, I've been unable to convince anyone that MY view is 'right' for them. I have explained, demanded, withheld, researched and re-explained, threatened, begged, withdrawn, and sulked. Yet, I keep looking for someone else to change to make me feel happier or at least better, safer, and 'righter'!

EXpectations are pre-planned misery, and their unique misery has devoured too much of my soul energy while playing unproductively in my consciousness.

I've tried quitting cold turkey and I've tried to 'affirm them away,' however eXpectations keep showing up to occupy my mind. Lately, I've noticed a red flag, though, a signal that an eXpectation wants to start playing. That red flag is a 'Why?' question:

"Why don't you do it this way?"
"Why are they always saying that?"
"Why is she choosing him?"
"Why won't he listen to me?"

When I hear myself ask a 'Why?' question, I take 3 seconds to breathe and then choose whether or not to let it drive me crazy, because mind you, these aren't real questions — these are eXpectations!

Do I have the right to eXpect others to listen to me; to do it my way; to love me; to trust me; to be kind, understanding, polite, generous, or safe; to basically do what I want them to do and be who I want them to be? Even if it's for their own good?

I used to think so, because I usually think I'm right. In fact, I AM right, however I'm only 'right' FOR ME.

How self-centered to think that my way of life is right for anyone else! Too often I forget that my rules, my values are ONLY FOR ME. I have no right to throw them AT YOU, in the form of an eXpectation.

No exceptions!

As a child, I remember not liking how it felt when my parents threw eXpectations at me. They were often stated as threatening, disapproving remarks that confused me, so I was often afraid of being yelled at, humiliated, or hit, and I never really knew what I was supposed to be doing.

As an adult, a parent, and a teacher, I have been committed to finding a better motivator beyond fear, shame, and intimidation to meet eXpectations.

I took the time to inspect the word itself, to find a new perspective, and I discovered a key to unlock the mystery.

In Latin, 'spect' means 'to look,' as in SPECTators and SPECTacles. So when I INspect, I'm 'looking into' something, and when I have a PERspective, I'm 'looking through' the evidence to get a new view of it all.

EX means 'outside,' so when I have EXpectations, I'm 'looking outside' myself, to others, to have the solution to MY concerns. How futile is that? Especially when I can't make anyone do anything!

I've ceased fighting and I've waved the flag of surrender. That is, I am giving up this losing battle of EXpectations and moving to the winning side of INspectations.

Instead of looking outside myself, I'm looking inside for my solutions. I replace my 'Why?' questions with real questions that I can answer truthfully:

"Is this my business?"
"Has anyone asked for my opinion?"
"Are my actions in alignment with my values?"
"Is there a way to look at this from another point of view?"
"Has anyone asked me directly for help?"

When I feel my inner red flag waving, it's usually because I'm looking outside myself to find someone or something else to calm my inner turmoil. Instead, I can spend my time developing some fruitful INspectations and 'look inside myself' to discover what it is that I value, that I cherish, that I am NOT honoring, and I can do something about that.

Where do you look when you feel the frustrations of your eXpectations??

E
is for
Eat Fear

An abundance of Fear is being served right now. Many say Fear is something to avoid, so perhaps you're distancing yourself from everything, from everyone who is peddling Fear, because "It's just not good for you."

I keep my life, my plate, full of what I love: grateful friends; bright colors; a sense of awe; great lyrics; my friends' artistry; warmth and joy; vulnerability; loving conversations; compassionate acts of kindness; and a daily dollop of humor. Then why would I allow a space for Fear and its purported omnipotence to be a side dish on my plate?

I'm not referring to Danger, where it's necessary to realize the harm or tragedy of a situation and the need to take shelter, take precautions, or ask for help.

I'm speaking of the invisible attack of Fear on Human Beings It takes up real estate in our hearts and minds and strips us of our freedom of creativity, clear thought, peace of mind, serenity, and safety. And we usually don't know where it comes from.

Unexamined Fear collapses the imagination and makes it impossible to think sanely or breathe rhythmically or stand steadily

Some questions I ask to examine my Fear…

Have I taken the time to deconstruct my Fear?

What components give it a bitter taste, and which offer a sweetness I never knew was present?

What ingredients could offer me unknown, inner strength to carry forward along a new path?

Have I ever considered the possibility that I could find Love in Fear?

How do you Eat Fear?

How do you eat an elephant? …One bite at a time.

I've seen the word Fear broken down as acronyms:

<u>F</u>alse <u>E</u>vidence <u>A</u>ppearing <u>R</u>eal
<u>F</u>uture <u>E</u>vents <u>A</u>lready <u>R</u>uined
<u>F</u>ace <u>E</u>verything <u>A</u>nd <u>R</u>un

What if there is another way to break down Fear?

What if I break down Fear the way the human body breaks down food?

What if the roughage of its presence is fiber for the Soul?

What if there's a kernel of truth, a bite of 'yes,' in one small portion of Fear?

What if there is a morsel of a hidden blessing in Fear?

What if Fear actually nourishes us?

Please allow me to introduce you to my favorite digestive organ, the small intestine.

The interior of the coiled-up 20 feet of small intestine is covered in innumerable, tiny villi, or threadlike projections, serving to increase the surface area needed to inspect every single thing I put into my mouth.

The total square footage over which all sustenance passes is that of a football field!

The small intestine's ongoing, objective inspection happens regardless of what I eat: a locally grown salad of seven super greens; non-fat yogurt; a moldy piece of homemade bread; fresh mahimahi; organic vodka; SPAM; or a chocolate fudge lava cake.

No matter what I choose to put in my body, the small intestine welcomes it in — without judgment, without lecturing. It never smirks, makes a comment or a recommendation; never expresses disappointment, yells, shames, or blames.

The small intestine objectively observes with each villus and selects those bits of food that are nutritious for the human being who is digesting it and lets the rest pass on through.

I want to live my life as the small intestine: to spend my energy wisely — welcoming that which is nourishing, that which builds me up, that which feeds me, and allowing the rest to flow on by.

So I wonder, is Fear an addiction?

Do we crave more than is healthy?

Are we drawn more to the rush we get from knowing it's on our plate?

Are we willing to break the addiction by taking the time to inventory which ingredients are up-building and which we need to let pass on by?

Perhaps the more accurate acronym of Fear is:

Forgetting Everything's All Right!

Fear and Love cannot be present at the same time, so I fill my heart, my home, my car, and my purse with visual reminders of Love.

Among others, I carry tiny hors d'oeuvres forks in my purse, and I offer other human beings the chance to take small bites out of their Fear, instead of allowing it to devour them.

If you were to Eat Fear, digest what nourishes you, and let the rest move on, what would YOU do next?

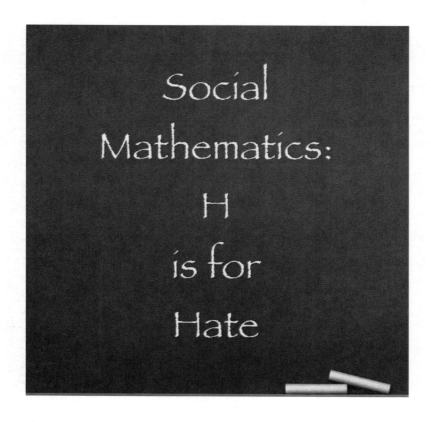

Social Mathematics #1

Algebra was one of the most surprisingly satisfying subjects to teach, for among the seemingly dry, strict processes and odd symbols were hidden, far-reaching, philosophical challenges.

I offered a mnemonic to my students to help them remember the appropriate signs for the answers when multiplying and dividing negative and positive numbers.

Love the Love	+	x	+	=	+
Love the Hate	+	x	-	=	-
Hate the Love	-	x	+	=	-
Hate the Hate	-	x	-	=	+

By replacing the words 'Love' with positive signs and the words 'Hate' with negative signs, the appropriate signs for the answers appear.

We all easily agreed that 'Loving the Love' was positive and that 'Loving the Hate' and 'Hating the Love' were negative.

When it came to 'Hating the Hate' though, mathematically we knew it was positive, however philosophically, I always left them with this question:

"Is, in fact, 'Hating the Hate' positive?"

In the language of mathematics, multiplying a negative times a negative indeed will give you a positive number. However, in the language of communication, of social artistry, does 'Hating the Hate' or having a negative impression of negative events generate positive energy?

Lately, I find myself 'Hating the Hate' to such an extreme that I find it difficult to recognize myself. I used to live like this all the time. My habit then was to be battle-ready, finding who was wrong, always knowing that I was right, then imagining some horrible action I would need to take to make everything settle down and return to normal.

I felt courageous with such powerfully negative thoughts! The root of courage is 'cor,' or 'heart' in Latin, and habitual reactions stem not from the heart but from well-worn, synaptic paths of fear in the unconscious mind. I've come to know that unconscious thought-habits are reactions and reactions are never courageous.

How I do one thing is how I do everything, and I want to lead from my heart.

So, if I cease focusing on what I am against, and I start focusing on what I am FOR, where will my heart lead me?

Rather than being paralyzed by 'Hating the Hate,' I can create a space within where something positive can grow.

I can pause, stop identifying what I think I am against, and start creating a heart-space where I can honor what I am FOR, practice my values, and begin to take new, positive actions.

Instead of being moved by my negative, unconscious thought-habits, I choose to be led by my heart to take action to be part of the positive change I want to see in the world.

I strive to be that kind of courageous where hating the hate can, in practice, become positive.

Social Mathematics:
I
is for
Integrity

Social Mathematics #2

Did you hate fractions?

Whether you did or not, hang with me, and I promise you'll have a fresh perspective on their role in your relationships — and you won't need to work a single math problem!

First, a few definitions, so we're all starting from the same place.

Say we have a whole pizza cut into 8 equal slices. If we give away 3 slices, we've given away ⅜ of the pizza and ⅝ of the pizza is left.

These are both Proper Fractions. Proper Fractions?!?

"So then, are there Improper Fractions?" you ask. Absolutely!

If we have more than 8 equal slices, say 21 slices, we can write this as 21/8. Writing it like this is called an Improper Fraction — a toppling tower of slices, quite improper and difficult to balance.

In math we find balance by redistributing the 'topple' into 2 whole pizzas with 5 slices leftover.

One whole pizza is made up of 8 equal slices. This wholeness can be written as a fraction as 8/8 or as an Integer as 1.

So now that we have a lexicon, let's see what fractions have to offer us on a social level.

On days when I feel my full value as a human, I feel completely present, and I have a sense of wholeness. I describe myself mathematically as feeling '1' or '8/8.' You might describe yourself as 11/11 or 243/243 or whatever is your favorite fractional-whole number.

As the Integer '1,' I can also describe myself as feeling whole, or Integrous, since both Integer and Integrity share the same root word.

On such days that I'm feeling not quite Integrous, less than whole, fractured, or as if a part of me is missing, I might feel $\frac{7}{8}$ or $\frac{3}{8}$ of myself.

When feeling a fraction of myself, I try not to make important decisions that require my full attention. I try to envision my perfectly normal, proper-fraction self, and I choose to be gentle, kind, loving, and supportive of myself, so I can heal into wholeness, back into my Integrity.

Then, there are those days when I feel overburdened, as if I'm carrying a toppling tower of pieces of life that are difficult to balance. I might feel 21/8 of myself.

On such days I witness myself rushed for time, overwhelmed, accusing others, or gritting my teeth for battle — all indicators of an improper-fraction self — and I try to allow for this perfectly normal occurrence of being out of balance.

So I pause and gently look for ways to delegate, to ask for help in redistributing some of the 'topple' in order to return to my Integrous self.

Not only am I an Agent of Integrity for my own behavior in the world, I can extend this form of Social Mathematics to others.

When I recognize that someone seems to be a bit off, a fraction of themself, I can be more consciously compassionate in my communications with them or even postpone engaging until later when they're more 'wholly' present.

Similarly, when I notice someone is seemingly snappish or rude, I can acknowledge they're out of balance today. Rather than judging their behavior or being insulted or injured by their less than stellar comments, I can instead remain compassionately quiet, not adding to their toppling tower, but ready to perceive an opportunity to ask, "How may I help?" or simply give them space to right themselves.

I strive to live in Integrity by being the first to acknowledge when I'm off-balance. As well, I strive to be an Agent of Integrity for those around me, actively ready at their request to help them find their way back into balance, into being fully human.

Just for fun, watch for the Social Mathematics in yourself as well as in others. What will you notice?

What is the 'measure' of your Integrity?

If you were to speak in fractions, how are you doing today?

L
is for
Like

Whether I'm playing in or out of the hodgepodge of social media options, some days I feel as though I'm living in a world where people 'like' to dislike things — fads, faces, fake news, foods — or they want me to 'like' what they're warning me about or 'like' what I should be afraid of.

From philosophy to gluten to political candidates to celebrities to farming practices to clothing styles, music, and movies, "I don't like this" is a common way humans are amassing armies, ready to do battle with one another in a blog.

It's as if dark clouds of complaint are growing in expansiveness, hovering over us all, casting shadows of hopelessness, worthlessness, and judgment, while blocking out any possibility for the light to be seen and considered.

There is a plethora of healing plants that have served the well-being of humans for lifetimes. Did you know that you can tell each plant's exact healing properties by its physical characteristics? I didn't.

For example, St John's Wort is a common indication for relieving the symptoms of depression, which often feels as though one is surrounded by a thick cloud of darkness that no light can penetrate.

Astonishingly, the leaves of the St John's Wort plant, when held up to the light, reveal minuscule holes, tiny punctures in the leaf, barely visible at first glance, yet enough to let light stream through the leaf.

I wonder if it would be possible to puncture the dark cloud of 'I don't like' with something that might permit the light of hope to seep in, no matter how gloomy the content, to make the weight of the words 'I don't like' work for us, so we can choose to live more in hope than in fear.

Remember the story of Saint George and the Dragon? A Medieval town is being terrorized by a dragon and no one seems able to slay it or make it go away. Then Saint George arrives, and with the light of his mighty sword, he is able NOT to slay it, but to subdue the dragon into working for the townspeople by pulling their plows and lightening their work.

I believe his power to transform came from 'liking' the dragon enough to find the possibilities of its usefulness, and in so doing, relieving the town of its doomed hopelessness.

What if we, too, are wielders of mighty word-swords of like-light?

What if we choose to bring our swords into the dark gloom of unconscious conversation and begin to transform it by spreading hope where there is despair?

There is a parable about Jesus walking with his disciples when they come upon the carcass of a dead dog. Although the disciples are consumed by all that they don't like about this situation, Jesus merely comments how beautiful are the dog's teeth!

Imagine spending one whole day, wherever your path takes you, speaking ONLY of that which you like.

What DO you like?

C
is for
Compost

I have dear friends who are biodynamic gardeners, and I was fortunate to raise my son on milk from a cow whose name he knew (Beverly) and meat from cows who were intentionally not named.

As partial payment for our seasonal harvest, we regularly weeded patches of the garden as members of the CSA (Community Supported Agriculture) and tossed our day's work into a huge compost pile.

I remember helping them move from one farm to another. The odd thing to me was that they did not transplant any of the crops. Those were left for the next farmer to harvest.

Instead we carefully moved an array of seedlings, starts, and unplanted fruit trees, and the most treasured commodity on the farm — the compost.

The compost consisted of years and years of past crops, cleared brush, unused scraps, unknown organic matter, and leftovers.

Between the pitchforks and the chickens, the pile would be turned over and over and over, and with time, that which had appeared to be unwanted garbage was transformed into a secret substance that promoted new life.

It was an example of ancient alchemy right before our eyes, the turning of lead into gold, for my friends referred to it as their 'gold.' According to them, the compost embodied that which would enable their future farm, more than anything else, to be more immediately verdant and productive.

I wonder, what if I were to take all my past experiences, cleared away hurts and heartaches, unused opportunities, mistakes, and leftover life events and put them into a pile?

I would certainly need to turn them over and over and over. However, by that I do not mean to analyze them ad nauseam. As with a tossed banana peel, if I keep pulling it out to identify it as a banana peel, it will never have the chance to break down into a useful substance.

In the same way, I would need to figuratively turn my pile over and over to allow the peels, labels, and details to dissolve, so they were no longer recognizable or visible to my mind's eye. I'd have to leave them alone to be magically transformed.

Would I, then, have a personal pile of compost, a golden pile of possibilities, from which to create new life?

Would this activity of turning over create a soul-mulch ready to receive the new seedlings, starts, and unplanted fruit trees of my hopes and dreams?

Could I transform the mistakes of the past into that which gives new life to a vintage relationship or a fresh start for a new beginning today?

I love the thought that my life is a pile of shit, and that my past is a transformable pile of experience and strength from which my hopes sprout forth. The truth is, my life keeps blooming and fruiting and getting better and better every day.

What old, useless, dead-weight memories, experiences, and beliefs would you like to toss into your compost pile?

Are you entirely ready for something new to sprout forth?

By the way, do you have a trusty pitchfork with which to turn over your compost pile?

P
is for
Pitchforks

When I have a pitchfork in my hand, I know exactly how to 'turn it over' — as in a compost pile, for example. However, when I'm dealing in the metaphorical realm, turning something over can be a huge inner challenge.

So I have created a plethora of pitchforks that I use at different times of day, for different situations, and each one works. Regardless of which pitchfork I choose, I keep in mind that pitchforks are not weapons for solving problems. They are tools to keep my mind calm, my side of the street clean, and my hands ready to do the next indicated thing, metaphorically speaking.

Here are 5 imaginations I use to 'turn it over.'

My Sunset Pitchfork

At bedtime, when I am haunted by worries and thoughts that simply won't allow me to fall asleep, I grab my Sunset Pitchfork. I imagine that I place all my cares in the setting sun, and that through the course of the night, they are burning and being transformed through a Fire Ceremony that takes place throughout the night while I'm sleeping, and I am not invited to attend!

When the sun rises, it brings shiny, new thoughts, new perspectives, and new ways to solve yesterday's worries, and I am better able to hear them because I have slept soundly through the night.

My Silver Pitchfork

On nights when I wake up in the middle of the night, an unexpected mind attack can arise with me. My worries taunt me to stay up and play with them. It's at this point that I draw on my Silver Pitchfork.

This pitchfork is the shape of a huge silver tray, and I literally lean over and imagine dumping out the full contents of my mind onto the tray — no sorting of any kind is necessary. Once my mind feels empty, I lift the silver tray over my head and ask all unseen beings on night-watch — all the Angels of Grace and other spiritual beings who respectfully wait for me to ask for their help — to inventory, declutter, and take care of this 'thought-booty' of mine so that I can get back to my real job — getting a full night's sleep.

I must confess, some nights I need to reach for my Silver Pitchfork multiple times, and I can report that no matter how many times I grab it, it works.

My Matador Pitchfork

There have been times during the course of the day when an unsuspected attack makes me feel as though I need to step out of its way. Granted, this is a different kind of turning over; it's the kind of turning over where I recognize that this charging bull is not mine. Therefore it is none of my business, and I need not engage with it.

I imagine I am a matador — my waistcoat bedazzled in rhinestones and sequins and my flashy cape flowing in the breeze. As the attack comes, I quickly step to the side and watch the bullish remarks run right past me. Then I smile, noting two things: I am unscathed and I look magnificent!

My 1° Pitchfork

The presence of the miraculous is woven throughout the science of astronomy. For example, our sweet planet is tilted at 23 1/2° and remains tilted at that degree throughout the year as it travels around our sun. The miracle is that if it were tilted 1° more, in either direction, at some point during the course of the year, our planet would either burn or freeze. Just a 1° shift would have an effect on all of us.

When I remember the powerful science of that statement, I more confidently turn over my current stance in a seemingly immovable discussion, without feeling I'm going to lose. I can choose to shift my point of view by 1° in conversations and interactions, especially in those that may feel unfriendly, confrontational, or even volatile. All I have to do is shift my own perspective by 1°, and the potential for everything to change is now a new option.

My Shadow Pitchfork

I remember an old VCR movie case with an image of a tiny man casting a huge, menacing shadow behind him. Some days I feel my judgmental thoughts are following me around like that, looming 10x larger than they actually are. I can forget they are merely shadows, not reality.

So I turn to face them, and with my fearless glance, I gradually shrink the shadows to fit into the palm of my hand. Then I take a deep breath and I blow them away.

Here's hoping these tools will help you turn over whatever it is you need to release.

Which one looks most useful to you?

F
is for
Fore-give

A friend asked me about my thoughts on forgiveness.

He had heard that the answer to his emotional unrest would be solved by finding forgiveness for the person whom he believed had harmed him in the past. He had tried for years and had been unsuccessful.

So he asked me what I thought about forgiveness. I immediately responded:

"I don't believe in forgiveness."

I don't believe in forgiveness and here is why...

I don't believe humans know what to do with forgiveness. I believe forgiveness is a spiritual gift.

I will never know what you are thinking when you do what you do. I only (barely) know what I'm thinking when I do what I do. So I don't have access to all the information I need to forgive you.

Scotland invented the game of golf, and for centuries an alert has been called out prior to the swing of the club: "Fore!" I imagine this is related to the prefix, 'FOR.'

So when I even consider 'FOR-giving' someone, I first hear the prefix of the word as a warning to alert myself to the potentially judgmental, condescending, or unbalanced path my thoughts or words are about to follow.

Instead, I pause to 'give' myself a new way to perceive the situation that appears to need forgiveness. I imagine being given a 'do-over,' and to prepare for that, I want to put some new responses in my back pocket. That way I can replay the situation and reach into my pocket to 'FORE-give' myself a new response.

This kind of 'FORE-give-ness' has worked for me time and again, and no one needs to change their actions or their opinion of me in order for it to work. I simply get to move forward with my life, repurposing challenges from my past to make my future better.

In place of the word forgive, I offer the word 'amend.'

When the course of my life veers off and upsets your world, I can choose to apply a nautical term, 'amend,' which is used by the Navigator when a ship veers off-course and needs to get back on-course. I can best amend my course when I say something such as:

"Please excuse me for not honoring your point of view."
"Please excuse me for my self-centeredness in thinking only my viewpoint is valid."
"Please excuse me for my fear that you were going to take away or not give me something I needed."
"Please excuse me for holding an unexamined assumption about who you are and how you react."

Whether or not these attempts to 'right my course' are accepted by the other person, I am better prepared to face a similar situation next time my ship veers off-course.

This practice of amending my own words or actions rather than forgiving others for their words or actions has made me a better Captain of my own life.

When do you find yourself 'off-course'?

Before you find yourself there again, what amended words or actions could you put in your back pocket to have ready if the situation arises again?

What would you FORE-give yourself?

S
is for
Sandpaper
Angels

Long ago I was invited to imagine that everyone who shows up in my life is bearing a gift, and it's my job to recognize the gift, be willing to receive it, and be grateful for it.

In some cases it's pretty easy to identify the gift. My son, for example, has taught me how to parent differently from how I was parented. Through my striving to choose response rather than reaction to the challenges he brought me, I was guided to bring out, respectfully and consistently, the inner excellence in him, and I am grateful for the gift of his presence in my life.

Some folks have modeled patience, open mindedness, joy, stability, and adventurousness.

While others have disappointed with their seeming unkindness, thoughtlessness, or harmfulness, or with their lack of professionalism, courage, or respect. For these folks, it's sometimes challenging to find the gift they brought me. However it is not impossible and often worth the effort.

Many have led me to discover my own unconscious self-centeredness, dishonesty, resentment, and fear.

One of my favorite children's books is *The Little Soul and The Sun* by Neil Donald Walsh. It concludes with the last line:

"Remember, I have sent you nothing but angels."

Most days I witness innumerable examples of human beings showing up for one another, as Angels, offering a kind word, a shared abundance, a place to stay, an ear, a space in traffic, a shoulder to cry on, or a word of encouragement.

Then there are other days...

I remember those with whom I've experienced disheartening relationships, abusive situations, or debilitating hardships and I remember the roughness of communication in those moments.

Squirming inwardly, struggling to find my words, every turn of a conversation felt abrasive, even cutting, as though I were being whittled away from my authentic core.

Not only do I find similar difficult relationships present in my life today, some have taken up rent in my mind for years, giving birth to chronic resentments that serve no purpose other than to eat away at my own energy.

To clarify, resentment is not a synonym for anger. It comes from the root word 'sentir' meaning 'to sense or feel' and 're' meaning 'again.' So any feeling that simply arises again and again is a resentment.

When I notice a recurring need to feel angry or ashamed or to label another or to find out who is at fault, I'm experiencing an unresolved resentment, and I'm more likely to see a Bad Guy, not an Angel, before me.

When I choose to move beyond the abrasiveness of others, I recognize within myself a new layer of courage, of authenticity waiting to be revealed. I find a new belief in myself, a strength to stand up for myself, for my ideas, and for my ideals.

I call such folks Sandpaper Angels, sent as gifts to help uncover something within myself.

As gifts, they present opportunities for me to experience transformative powers:

~ of choice, when I consciously choose my responses;

~ of time, when I pause before speaking too quickly;

~ of perspective, when I recognize the 'yes' in what
they're offering; and,

~ of an open mind, when I'm free of judgment.

If you were to stand 1" to the side of a current situation where communication is rough and look anew, could you see how this person's presence is awakening you to an inner knowing about yourself?

Can you see how their presence is whittling away old beliefs that are keeping you trapped in behaviors that no longer serve you highest self?

Think of someone in your life who has served as a Sandpaper Angel.

Take a moment to thank them inwardly.

Over time, notice how the lingering sting of their seeming abrasiveness is replaced by gratitude for the awakening their 'sandpaper' has revealed in you.

Y
is for
You're So
Cute!

Dog lovers amaze me. I have witnessed perfectly rational humans come home to discover their favorite shoes, pillow, or shirt slobbered up and shredded by their unpredictable puppy.

Sure, there's some high-pitched yelling, however, it's only in grieving the 'death' of these belongings.

Rarely is there any anger or even disappointment aimed at the dog. Instead the sweetest voice comes forth to say to the puppy, "You're so cute!"

Such a vision, such kindness, such open-heartedness, such willingness to hold a mishap in a right-sized perspective. Dog lovers are unabashed practitioners of unconditional love towards their furry family members.

I want to be seen, spoken to, judged, and loved in that way!

By comparison, when I make the tiniest of mistakes — making a wrong turn, burning the rice, or forgetting to return a call or start the dryer — I often blow such indiscretions out of proportion and speak inwardly to myself in an unbelievably derogatory tone, lashing out:

"God, Penni, are you really that stupid?!"
"Now look what you've done! You're so thoughtless!"
"You @#! idiot! What a mess! You're hopeless!"

I shudder to think I would ever speak to anyone in this way, yet here I am.

In admitting these examples of how I speak to myself when reacting to a challenge, can I really claim to be a practitioner of self-love? What I'm actually practicing in these moments is self-loathing, self-ridicule, and self-deceit.

Time to take my thought-life to Obedience School!

My habitual self-talk was sarcastic, mean-spirited, and out of balance with the transgression. I spoke to myself as if what I'd just done (usually a pretty minor human infraction) was a mortal sin, a violation of some imaginary code of perfection that I believed deserved humiliation and punishment, and I was the inner judge, jury, and executioner.

Admittedly, that's overly dramatic, however, when you really look at the harsh words I was unconsciously choosing, I was a bully!

Most mishaps are usually something I do repeatedly, almost unconsciously, as with the dog and the shoe, and yet the dog receives unconditional love and I get bullied.

I've chosen to reframe how I speak to myself when mishaps occur. I consciously choose to be more 'honest,' that is, I choose to 'honor' the truth, scope, and importance of the issue at hand, and allow 'simple human error' to be a choice more aligned with the actual nature of the sin committed.

As for that word, 'sin,' it's an archery term that means 'to miss the mark,' and isn't that all I've done when I've missed a turn or forgotten a phone call?

Following the model of unconditional love set forth by dog-lovers, I now inwardly say to myself, "You're so Cute!"

I even have "You're so Cute!" programmed into my GPS app for when I don't follow the driving directions exactly. The words come on so often when I'm at the wheel that one dear friend has forbidden me to use it because, as he says, "I just don't need to keep hearing about how cute you are!"

Changing the way that I speak to myself has altered how I interact with the world. I directly experience myself as kinder and more patient, a better listener, more tolerant, understanding, and peaceful, and a better friend, mother, and human being.

As a result, what matters most to me is not what you're reading, how you're eating, or for whom you're planning to vote. What matters most is how you treat yourself on the inside.

Are you a practitioner of unconditional love or are you a bully?

H is for 2020 Hindsight

Back in the 80's there was a TV show called Dallas. The whole country seemed concerned with the tragic-mystery that ended one season with the cliffhanger — "Who shot JR?"

I didn't watch much TV, yet from the daily 'water cooler conversations,' I was kept up-to-date over the course of the next season with the ever-changing details and opinions that kept the country engaged. So many opinions! No one solution satisfied all the thorny details and plot twists. The entire season was devoted to trying to find an answer to the question — "Who's to blame?"

When the series returned the following year, in the first scene of the first episode, one of the leading ladies rolled over in bed, and right beside her was none other than the character JR, unharmed, alive, and well. The way the writers explained it — the whole previous season had been a dream!

I admired the creativity of such a resolution. It allowed the cast and writers to spend an entire year examining the unspoken, unacknowledged beliefs, suspicions, prejudices, assumptions, expectations, and labels that the characters could so easily grab and fling at one another, and in the end, seemingly there were no consequences.

I must confess, I did not start watching the show to see if the characters transformed themselves with their newfound consciousness. However, when the memory of this 'dream solution' came up the other day, I had one burning question:

"What would happen if we all went to sleep this New Year's Eve and woke up on January 1, 2020 again? What if we discovered this whole past year had been a dream?"

Upon awakening, would we go back to working too many hours away from home, forgetting the precious opportunities we've spent with our children, our partners, and our pets?

Would we remember sneaking away from our usual commitments to fall back in love with our partners?

Would we still take time for our rediscovered pastimes and passions such as cooking, stained glass, writing poetry, drawing, singing, gardening, walking, and playing guitar?

Would we remember how deeply we missed our friends?

Would we remember how we yearned for a handshake or a hug or face-to-face eye contact, from strangers or even from people that we don't particularly like?

Would we remember how much a smile jumping out of the eyeballs of a masked someone we don't even know means during the course of a day?

At the end of the day, would we remember that, both in joy and in hardship, we are more alike than we are different?

Would we finally know that taking exquisite care of ourselves is the best way to heal the fear that ails us, whether dealing with health, relationships, or abundance?

Would we understand that fearful, disconnected human beings choose war, within and without?

Would we finally choose to stop being at war with everyone and everything and surrender to peace, remembering that surrender is not giving up — it's moving over to the winning side.

Would we choose to be imprisoned by relentless, fearful beliefs? Or would we awaken to new ways of being with one another?

Unlike the TV show, this is not a dream. It's not even a nightmare. It's simply the next in a series of life-challenges. How I choose to BE will make all the difference — to me and to others.

For me, this year has not been about figuring out who's to blame or even what's to blame. It's about remembering the values that have become self-evident. It's about making certain I live by those values from this day forward.

I want to be who I am at my core, at all times, with all beings, no matter what.

I want to wake up each day in fearless peace, with a certainty that a goodness I am not yet able to understand is taking care of me and everyone.

I have a choice. I can live in fear and distrust, constantly searching for "Who's to blame?" for whatever the current life-challenge is, or I can choose to be the fearlessly loving person I'm meant to be.

I have a choice and so do you. Who and how do you want to be, no matter what?

V is for Voices

I have spent a lifetime sorting through the various voices that occupy my mind. When I was younger, they were always pointing out how much better everyone else was than I. They told me you were watching and judging me, and I would never be enough unless I fought long and strong with everyone.

As I started accumulating life experiences, the voices started judging me for how or how much or how little I did or did not do. As the judgments began to weigh me down, I started limiting what I asked for, what I expected, what I did, and what I wanted to do.

I started believing the ever-increasing voices in my head:

"You're wrong. Shut up."
"You're a bad girl, and you'll get in trouble
    if you don't hide."
"You're so stupid. You should know better."
"You'll never be able to…"
"How could you have…?"

I accepted those words as accurate, all-knowing voices of truth. At some point, I even thought they were my higher-self speaking to me, trying to make me a better person. I mistakenly believed they were trustworthy principles by which to live.

I've come to know that voices of Negativity, Limitation, Scarcity, Ineptitude, and Mistrust try to distract my attention with degrading judgments. Only voices of Fear, Shame, Hatred, War, and Separateness lie to me like that.

That is not how the voice of Love or Peace or Grace speaks to me or to anyone.

My true inner voice speaks in principles of Kindness, Inclusivity, Patience, and Appreciation.

The voice of Love speaks in principles of 'YES' —

"Please wait. I'd like you to pause a while before you
make this decision."

"I hear your yearning, and there is someone else for you
to meet who will be just the person you're looking for."

"Congratulations. Saying 'no' to that request was a
courageous act and the best fit for this situation."

"Yes, I hear what you're asking, and my response at this
moment is not right now."

"Thank you for being patient. They may be wounded
more than you know."

"Breathe. This small voice within knows better than those
clanging gongs of self-doubt and blame."

This Voice of Truth is Unconditional Love. That is, Love with
absolutely NO CONDITIONS. It is the most powerful force and it
wins every time.

Take a moment and imagine what that kind of loving would
feel like—both to give and to receive Unconditional Love.

When my voices start spewing, the sooner I can remember the
truth of who I am and the truth of the principles I want to guide my
actions, the more chance I have of being the person I want to be... a
person guided by the higher principles I have chosen.

What are your inner voices saying to you?

Which Inner Voice do you choose to listen to?

F
is for
Further
Wonderings

When I was a student in high school, lab reports had to end with a conclusion, indicating that an experiment had proven a fact.

I know today that scientists do not deal in 'facts.' Instead, they deal in 'hypotheses' that keep them always questioning, percolating in their perspectives: "Given what I've just seen, where do I explore next?"

So when I instructed my own students on how to write up a lab report, I didn't ask for conclusions. I asked them instead, "With these results, what are the questions that have arisen that make you want to get back in the lab? What's the next experiment you want to do? What are your 'Further Wonderings'?"

Over time, I've become comfortable remaining in a state of continued questioning. I consider my inner games to be spiritually scientific soul experiments, and when I come to the end of one, I contemplate my 'Further Wonderings.'

Now it's your turn.

Now that you've played the inner games I've shared on the pages of this book, what kind of inner game would you like to play next?

When are you challenged to choose Peace?

What other kinds of War are showing up to taunt you?

Got any 'Yeh, buts…?'

Please let me know. I've got more games coming.

Thanks for playing.

Love, Penni

Penni's Lexicon of Power Words

and Where to Find Them

A is for Awake

'PAY' attention: Our attention is a valuable commodity that humans spend consciously or unconsciously.

A is for Armor

A smoke ring around the heart is an image to help stop smoking.

B is for Busy

'Busy': In Chinese, the word is made up of two glyphs: one is 'heart', the other is 'murdering.'

C is for Compost

My life is a pile of shit, and my past is a transformable pile of experience and strength from which my hopes sprout forth.

C is for Cows

'COWs': Watch out for: Conditions. Outcomes. War.

D is for Defuse

'HALT': An acronym for three states of being that affect our interactions with others: Hungry. Angry. Lonely. Tired.

3 Steps to Defusing a Social Bomb:
>   Thank you
>   Pardon me
>   Is there more?

E is for Eat Fear

'FEAR': An acronym for many 'states of being':
>   <u>F</u>alse <u>E</u>vidence <u>A</u>ppearing <u>R</u>eal
>   <u>F</u>ace <u>E</u>verything <u>A</u>nd <u>R</u>un
>   <u>F</u>uture <u>E</u>vents <u>A</u>lready <u>R</u>uined
>   <u>F</u>orgetting <u>E</u>verything's <u>A</u>ll <u>R</u>ight!

The small intestine: my favorite digestive organ.

F is for Fore-give

'Fore!': In golf, before you swing the club, this shout-out warns that something potentially dangerous is coming.

'Fore - Give': Give to yourself before this happens again.

'Amend' is a nautical term used to correct the ship's course.

F is for Further Wonderings
Scientists do not deal in 'facts;' instead they deal in 'hypotheses' that keep them always questioning.

H is for Hate
Mnemonic for answers to multiplying or dividing signed numbers

    Love the Love

    Love the Hate

    Hate the Love

    Hate the Hate

Courage comes from 'cor,' Latin for 'heart.'

H is for 2020 Hindsight
What would happen if we all went to sleep this New Year's Eve and woke up on January 1, 2020 again? What if we discovered this whole past year had been a dream?

H is for Huli
'Ho'oponopono' is a spiritual Hawaiian practice of removing hindrances that block you from moving forward.

I is for Imagine
'Ignorance' come from 'ignore;' it does not mean 'stupid.'

I is for Integrity

'Proper fractions' & 'Improper fractions' are clues for checking your inner soul mathematics.

An 'integer' is a whole number and is the root of 'integrity' meaning 'wholeness.'

L is for Like

St. John's Wart looks like that which it is meant to heal.

M is for Magnet

A 'magnet' is magnetite from Magnesia; it is not related to 'attraction.'

'Serenity' comes from 'serene,' a 'title of high nobility.'

P is for Peace

WAIT: An acronym for Why Am I Talking?

P is for Pitchforks

For help with 'turning it over,' I have 5 pitchforks to choose from:

> Sunset Pitchfork
>
> Silver Pitchfork
>
> Matador Pitchfork
>
> 1° Pitchfork
>
> Shadow Pitchfork

R is for Red Ink Letters
Hurt people hurt people.

S is for Sandpaper Angels
'Resent' is from 'sentir,' 'to feel' and 're,' 'again.' It is not a synonym for 'being angry.'

S is for Spiritual Food Groups
'Sanos' is 'health or balance' as in sanitarium or sanity. It is not synonym for 'crazy.'

4 Spiritual Food Groups: Connect, Self-care, Serve, Play

S is for Stars
Star Game: Getting Caught in the Act of Doing Something GOOD, not well.

T is for Three Seconds
'Sarcasm' comes from 'sarkos' meaning 'to strip off the flesh.' "Isn't that interesting?"

V is for Vertical
'Reconnecting' comes from 'religare,' the Latin root word of 'religion.'

V is for Voices

The voice of Love speaks in the principles of 'YES.'

X is for eXpectations

In Latin:

'spect' means 'to look.'

'ex' means 'outside of.'

So...an 'expectation' is 'to look outside of' myself

'per' means 'through.'

So...a 'perspective' is 'to look through' everything.

'in' means 'in.'

So....an 'in-spectation' could mean 'to look inside.'

(OK, 'inspection' works, too.)

Y is for You're So Cute!

'Unconditional' is 'no conditions.'

'Honesty' is connected to 'honor.'

'Dis-honesty' is connected to 'dis-honoring.'

'Sin' is an archery term meaning 'to miss the mark.'

P is for Penni

Penni Sparks is a Wayfinder and Hindrance Remover for those who feel lost, stuck, or are looking for a new perspective.

She is also an educator, consultant, personal coach, keynote speaker, facilitator, mentor, Judo instructor, observational astronomer, choir director, whitewater canoeist, director/choreographer, celestial navigator, Zumba enthusiast, linguistics nerd, and author.

Penni's unique approach is inspirational and has been honed over 30+ years of experience leading empowerment workshops, dedicated to inspiring human beings to greater confidence and kindness.

The popularity of her workshops — and Penni's dynamic brand of encouraging adults to take up their own inner work — has led her to become a sought after speaker across the country.

An Ohio University alum, Penni holds a BA in French and German with a minor in Art History. Her Master's thesis in Linguistics supplied the syntax and grammar for the Algerian dialect of Arabic. She is a veteran Waldorf teacher and has practiced various and anonymous spiritual activities for over 40 years.

Penni lives on the side of a volcano overlooking the ocean in Kailua Kona on the Big Island of Hawaii. She is friend-rich, however, her best friend is her son, Alexander, an accomplished concept artist in LA.

With warmth and humor, Penni invites you into your finer self to play her inner peace games, *The ABC's of Being Human*.

Made in the USA
Columbia, SC
23 May 2023

16644261R00075